~ Business By Jesus ~

~ Business By Jesus ~

SHN
PO Box 26506
Glasgow
G74 9DJ
Scotland
United Kingdom

www.shnpublishing.com

A catalogue record of this book is available from the
British Library.

ISBN 978-0-9557608-7-7

Text © Kevin Cameron
Illustrations © Leanne Hamilton

Business by Jesus

Written by

Kevin Cameron

For Dad

I'm always reaching for the stars.

Contents

Important

Firstly, before you settle down and read this book, I must explain something quite important: I am not Salman Rushdie. I don't really want to spend the rest of my days hiding from religious fanatics who take offence at my book. I do not claim to be God, a God, the messiah or your saviour.

If you don't like the book I suggest you burn it. The paper is extremely flammable. If you borrowed this book then buy a copy and burn that one. Buy more and burn them too if you want. I'll arrange a discount for bulk burnings.

They say, "God created man in his own image." Hopefully that means with a sense of humour. Perhaps God looks like you. That would be funny. This book has nothing to do with religion. God will receive no fee.

Business by Jesus is my book. If you bought the book, thank you. I eat because of you.

Introduction

I must have read every business book there is. Bio-graphies from every tycoon litter my bookshelves. I needed to understand how to become one. How do I get from me to mogul in one easy step? I wanted riches and fame, mostly my own private plane, but I'd start with riches. I wanted my brain to be used and my ideas to flourish. Donald Trump was going to call me and I'd be too busy to take his call.

Every business book tells the same story. Some guy or girl in the right place at the right time was lucky. Some had the benefit of family money to start (which has never been a guarantee of success). Others struggled to raise the funding or get people to believe in their product. Every success story has the same message, the never ending self belief of the entrepreneur. Most of the books follow a very similar path. There are few (if any) simple books which guide the reader through the pitfalls of starting a business.

There are thousands of theories and ideas around to help you fight against your competitors. You have the talent and tenacity to beat all of them. To win is sim-ple; you only need to know how to run the most suc-cessful business ever! If you can understand how to do that, you can beat everyone.

Business is nothing new, or complicated.
If this was the usual complicated business book I'd

say "Business improvement thrives on the evolution of ideas; it needs fuel to survive, it requires continuous fine-tuning, there is consistent development of the marketplace. The business responds to cyclic activity as a result of organic customer maturity. The customer demographics must be strategically targeted to advance the development plan."

But don't panic, complications are only brought about by snot-nosed managers who have attended courses and learned big words. If business was that tricky no one would survive.

Have you any idea how much money is made by consultants, advisors and experts pretending business is a new complicated phenomenon? All they are doing is following the simple rules that have applied since the dawn of time. This book will save you the expense of consultants.

Whether you are planning a new venture or looking for ways to improve your existing business, my hope is that this book will help in offering clear, simple advice from the best business book ever written...

The Bible can teach you everything you need to know about business.

In simple terms, business is getting what you want by giving what you have. It's that basic. I could end the book here but it would just be a pamphlet. To really understand, we should look back to the man who brought business to us on a grand scale. The world's first successful franchise operator and true entrepreneurial genius – Jesus.

This book is not a book about religion, the Church or the rights and wrongs of any faith. It is about using lessons from the past to shape your business and increase your profits to Biblical proportions.

In the Beginning,
Commerce Commenced

Before Jesus was around, business was simple. Ancient civilisations formed businesses where people sold their strengths. Picture the scene, little Johnny is the fastest runner in the tribe. He can out run nearly all the buffalo. Sprints like a dream and can catch an animal quikker than anyone else, but he can't use a knife, he's hopeless. His friend William One Leg sadly was involved in an accident with a large bison and can no longer run (except in circles). He can, however, cut and skin a buffalo in minutes. A business is formed. Johnny trades his skill for William's skill. Without each other they both starve. See how easy that was?

No marketing, no pressure, no competition; until Sammy Smartarse comes along. He can run and skin animals with half the labour costs. Do you see where this is going? William One Leg and Little Johnny have to raise their game and compete or starve. Modern managers would have a time and motion study here. They'd draw graphs and talk you to death but I'm sure you already get the picture.

The higher cost business is forced out by the one with lower overheads. Unless William and Johnny can develop their business to compete they will starve, so they add value by soaking the buffalo meat in wine which they sell as, 'luxury, wine infused buffalo steaks'

– at a premium price. Once again, they are market leaders, and so it goes on.

For your business:

- People need to want what you offer.
- There needs to be sufficient demand

Ask every day if the above statements are true!
The needs of the customer do change; sometimes slowly, sometimes quickly.

If you ask every day if people need what you offer, if you check every day if there is sufficient demand for your product/service, you will always be a step ahead of your competition.

So, in the beginning business was simple, supply and demand. You're probably wondering when Jesus comes into this. He's on the way. I'm just setting the scene for his arrival.

Jesus wasn't the first businessman, but he was the first star entrepreneur.

The Virgin Empire

Mary was the original brains behind the Jesus operation. She was the one who saw the potential for her son. It was She who started the Virgin Mary whispers and put about the story that she was to give birth to the son of God. Why did she do this? She risked ridicule for her stories but she kept on with the same line. She was to be the mother to the son of God. Like any business plan, many people will think you are nuts, but keep on if you believe in the plan yourself. You will only succeed through your belief.

Mary needed investment for what was to be a family business. To some, she was clearly crazy, but she kept on with the story until she got what she wanted: investment.

Enter the three wise men; original investors in the Jesus corporation. Gold, frankincense and myrrh were all worth a fair amount in those days. It was Mary who called them the three wise men. Wise because they had believed in her. What a great investment they made. They were to be known throughout their lives as wise men and set up the world's first business consulting agency, going on to make millions.

Mary had convinced these guys to part with their wealth, as the prophets had foretold of the coming of the messiah. For it would be her son who would reap the benefits of that prophecy.

It's odd that the Bible never mentions what happened to the wealth; perhaps it was used to train and educate Jesus to be the son of God. By the time he was ready to face the world, Jesus was already streets ahead of everyone around him. Like many parents of entrepreneurs, his mother had made sure he knew he was special, different and able to do anything he wanted. If he failed, he apparently had his carpentry to fall back on.

Mary planted the seeds in Jesus' mind which enabled him to formulate a plan to become the world's most successful entrepreneur.

Jesus got the picture. Carpenter my arse. Tycoon of Nazareth more like. Have you ever heard of Jesus measuring up a job? Finishing a cabinet? He couldn't be bothered. The first time he was close to a hammer it was nailing him to the cross. Jesus was too lazy to be a carpenter. That's the first rule of business. Manuel Labour is a bloke from Spain.

No tycoon ever got anywhere working. Go read the Bible; if you find *"Jesus pondered as he formed the dove-tail joint"*, I'll give you a free holiday in the Holy Land. He didn't know his ash from his ebony.

If you work like a peasant, you will stay a peasant. Most people are too busy working to make money. They have responsibilities like a mortgage, debt payments, family etc. They become trapped by the fear of having insufficient income to meet their commitments. They choose a job they dislike for money they need.

Jesus had better ideas. He was, after all, the world's first marketing genius. Jesus knew he had to find a business – and fast. He had to build an empire which could bring in cash, feed him and offer stability. He had to choose something which would stop him having to really graft for his daily bread. He realised it had to be something which appealed to everyone. Life expectancy 2000 years ago was a little short. Seeing your grandchildren was almost unheard of, in fact, seeing your own children was often a bonus. Death frequented the towns and villages, touching the young and old alike. That's it – death, it's a sure thing. Everyone dies.

Business plans happen like that. Eureka moments in the bath or on the golf course, (although I'm not sure Jesus was a golfer). They NEVER happen if you are too busy working. If he really had been a carpenter, Jesus would have been too busy with his wood to let his mind stray. That's also why Pee Wee Herman is no tycoon.

A business plan can be a simple idea. Most people let the idea die. Only true entrepreneurs go to the next level. They daydream. I know that the school you went to said the opposite, but remember, schools are conditioning you to be normal, not entrepreneurial. Daydream, plan, imagine. See your success. Jesus did just that.

Death was the business. "Everyone dies. Death is scary; no one knows what happens next. We have this uncertainty we can build on." By now, Jesus was excited; thinking and planning the business. "Every business is the same," he thought. "How do we sell death?"

Essentially, we're all the same. Everyone is born and everyone dies. The only difference is the variable time in between. None of us know how long we have. You could be reading this on the train or the plane. Statistically, you should be fine; please don't worry; I'm sure all the noises you are hearing are perfectly normal. That cough you heard might not contain harmful bacteria, which would penetrate your immune system. You'll be fine for now. One hundred percent of the people reading this will die though…but perhaps not today.

Death is a tough sell; it's unwelcome, frightening and at times horrific. Jesus had a problem. He had worked out that everyone dies, so everyone had a need, but how could he turn that into a business? Death is a very negative thing; it has no positive aspects at all.

Had Jesus listened to his friends, or had he conducted a survey, he would have been advised against proceeding. Every entrepreneur is faced with family and friends bringing a good idea to its knees. It is always good practise to get opinions on any new concept and think them through but if you believe in the project, you can make it work. There is always, always a way.

"Let's make it a new beginning, a fresh start; after all, we're hardly going to get anyone to prove us wrong are we? We can make death the entrance to a kingdom of untold riches, far beyond known wealth."

Jesus had just given one of his first lessons: re-branding.

Only ever re-brand negative images to positive ones.

Jesus knew about re-branding 2000 years ago. A few years ago, in the UK, the Royal Mail, one of the most famous institutions in the world started calling itself 'Consignia'. What the hell for? What does it mean? Why? Jesus wouldn't have done that. The person who dreamt that one up would probably want to put Coca Cola in green cans with a different name or something.

Never ever re-brand a seller. Imagine all those business leaders who wanted to make their brand into a worldwide recognised name, only for some wet behind the ears graduate to change it to something no one has heard of. Leave a worldwide brand alone.

British Airways. What were they thinking with the tail-fin logos? I could have told them in one minute it wouldn't work. BA tail fins were a strong visual symbol all over the world, 'flying the flag'. Who scrapped them and why? Why didn't someone stop them?

If only they had looked to Jesus. Corporate image is the biggest asset of any company and should never be diluted or cheapened in any way. Alterations should only be made to enhance a brand.

So, Jesus began to re-design an age-old product: death. You start any new business in the same way. Put your idea in the middle and let it become the centre; stare at it in your mind. Daydream and see what direction your mind takes you.

"We could make death glamorous. Make people feel like we are giving them a service. In fact, that's good – a death service. That doesn't sound right though, death, bereavement, demise, no…there must be something. Hold on... memorial service. That's it, lets have a burial service where we let the deceased enter the kingdom of riches. Without the service they would suffer some kind of horrible fate. We've got to make the people scared not to go with us."

Of course ritual and burial was nothing new. Every culture had one. Even ancient Vikings and Egyptians all had some type of death ritual. Jesus just brought together the best of everything. But that was only death, what about life? Expand your idea. Look at all the permutations. Daydream again. When you stared out that classroom window you were already showing entrepreneurial spirit. Unless, of course, you were checking out the netball team. If someone says you are a dreamer, thank him or her. So it's good to dream? Of course it is. Dreamers make dreams come true.

Imagine life is a journey from wherever you are to the Eiffel Tower. For everyone, that journey, like life, is a different length. Short for the French – but then they charged me £12 for a beer so to hell with them. Robbing, thieving bandits! Dick Turpin was nicer. Anyway. from where you are to the Eiffel Tower is your life. Say you are in Los Angeles. Would you go straight to Paris without stopping in Vegas, New York or London if the opportunity was there? Would you close your eyes as you passed the Arc de Triumph? Of course you wouldn't. Don't close your eyes to life. Make your journey count. Take it all in.

Jesus had a journey; not the longest on record, but a journey, nonetheless. His journey mattered. He was the most successful entrepreneur of all time. He was the first real icon, he understood show business, how to get a crowd and how to merchandise. Christmas and Easter were just part of what he left for us.

Jesus is a better businessman than Ronald McDonald, Bill Gates and Richard Branson put together. He is a bigger star than Elvis ever was. John Lennon may have thought he was bigger; he was certainly a better songwriter, but as an icon, Jesus beats them all. He has more influence and a bigger audience than anyone ever could. But he's been clever. We will examine how Jesus got to where he did, how he became an icon and how he operated the business with steely precision.

Son of God

It was an easy claim.

Today, you'd be laughed out of town, but 2000 years ago things were different. Mary wanted Jesus to reach as high as he could and be as bold as possible. The idea was marketing; marketing wasn't new. Romans, Aztecs, Egyptians had all been able to market ideas. You don't build a pyramid or a Roman fort without first convincing people they need one. Ok, so you round up a few slaves and beat the crap out of them till they build it. First you have to convince someone there is a need. The slaves´ need is to get through another day without being killed. Keeping one's body intact is a highly marketable concept.

Marketing is simply selling a need. Convince someone they can't do without your product or service. Let them see what you are offering.

"Son of God, what him?" The whispering had begun and Jesus was getting known. "Hey, that guy thinks he's the Son of God." The ancient texts had written that the Messiah would come; Mary thought it should be Jesus.

Jesus could've said: "Mum you're nuts, get help." However he used the situation to his advantage. This showed what set Jesus apart from others. He put every situation to his advantage and took the best from it.

"Rather than prove to the people I am the Son of God, prove I'm not…"

This showed early genius. Jesus was a big thinker and a clever one. He was marketing himself as God's earthly ambassador. Who could argue? People were afraid of death, they needed reassurance. Who better than God's son to reassure the people, and make money? Jesus was able to build his company using this as the cornerstone of his business.

If you are looking to market your product or service, follow the example of Jesus. If you can't prove the facts make sure no one else can disprove your facts. If it's ice cream you sell which is just the same as everyone else's then market it better in some way. Find a hook. Was it Elvis Presley's favourite? Well it is now!

Many entrepreneurs start small, building up larger and larger as time goes on. Jesus was the same, not the humble carpenter as the stories have us believe, but a business legend. Preaching, getting the company message out, telling the public what they wanted to hear and finding a following.

It's still the same today,

- Find a following for your business and keep them coming back.

How much do companies spend on experts to tell them this every year? It's not rocket science. It's basic.

If you've started a business, you stand on your soap box and preach. Sell your company's message to the people, the investors and yourself. Your business plan becomes a Bible and you live by it every day, selling the beliefs and ideals of your company. Picture in your mind Jesus preaching to his flock. He had a big message to sell so widened the coverage by bringing in staff, disciples, to spread his message for him – and advertising was born.

Today we have millions of media channels to choose from. This makes advertising difficult and costly, but we can look at that in more detail later. The best channel for advertising is the same one Jesus used all those years ago: word of mouth. Cheap, highly effective and the easiest way to get your message across the way you want. Become something to talk about.

Being in control of your message and image is one of the most important aspects of business. Jesus had to create the image of a new forward-thinking business; he had to make you believe that you had to follow his will. He had to make you believe it was your decision and will to part with your money. Here we see more genius. Jesus made people believe that money was unimportant and in fact, undesirable. It is easier to pass a camel through the eye of a needle than a rich man to enter the kingdom of heaven…in other words, you can have all the benefits of my service, it is more important than your cash so you may as well let me look after your cash for you.

What Jesus was saying, in effect, was, "My service is one your money cannot afford. You are not rich enough for my services." Stella Artois is a reassuringly expensive beer for a reason, to make you believe you are worthy of it, no matter the cost, making the cash of secondary importance.

Jesus was making you feel that you had to have his services and you would stop at nothing to get them.

It was image building or branding.

"If we can make the people believe we don't want their money, they will gladly give it".

Imagine the whispering, the gossip, the pitch – this guy doesn't want your money he wants to help you for no reward, he wants no money he's on my side, what a trustworthy guy! After all, he's the Son of God! Now think of a collection plate, what's it for?

Double glazing companies call you up and have selected your home to appear in their brochure and they will pay you a fee for the endorsement. Well that's not really the full picture but you are sucked in before you find out the true cost. Human nature won't let you back out as you may look foolish. Jesus was letting you have his service free, or was he? Genius, sheer genius.

Becoming the Celebrity

Sir Richard Branson, Donald Trump and Bill Gates are all celebrity tycoons, but Jesus was the first. Contacts can help any business start. It would be much easier for Donald Trump to get through to the chairman of the world's largest bank than it would for me. That's because of his celebrity status. I'd get through to the secretary of the personal assistant to his secretary's personal assistant and that would be on a good day.

Jesus knew fame would help spread his message (as well as help to get girls, good tables at restaurants and discounts on all manner of things). His fame would also add to the reputation of his business empire. The claim 'Son of God' gave him that status. What Jesus wanted was to build an empire which would allow him to be famous and to develop sources of income for his business.

How could Jesus get his fame? He had to become the world's first celebrity. He had to convince people that he was important, that he was the Son of God. Jesus was a genius. He made sure all the people who surrounded him were passing on his message – like modern-day celebrities, he travelled in convoys of people with his minders surrounding him. These days when you see a celebrity getting out of a limousine and going into a star-studded event, think of Jesus walking through Jerusalem, surrounded by his many fans. Essentially, it's the same thing.

Donald Trump often walks through Atlantic City surrounded by minders, whereas, other casino bosses and celebrities travel unhindered along the boardwalk. Donald Trump knows how to create the appearance of fame and the fantasy of importance.

Most businesses require an image to be created. Not necessarily a true image, but certainly one which reflects a status for the business.

When a salesman turns up at your door to sell you a kitchen in his battered old Ford, he is unlikely to get the sale because you don't trust him. This is because of his car and the image it projects. Alternatively, if the man turns up in a flashy sports car, he is probably already spending far too much of your money.

A balance has to be struck with the right image for the right task within the business. Jesus was trying to create the image of a poor, but popular, man. He did this by wearing shabby clothes and surrounding himself with followers that helped him to appear poor.

He had no home or food and relied on the generosity of others to see to his needs. This, again, helped him appear poor.

Jesus was a poor man with no worldly goods, promising you the riches of heaven. His point was that all the gold on earth was worthless. Your ticket to true wealth was only being sold through him. Had he been wearing the ancient equivalent of an Armani suit, wouldn't his sales pitch have been a little harder to swallow?

Lesson from Jesus:

Match your own image and that of your company to your product.

Reach for the sky

Here's a picture for you. Go to any town or city even fifty years ago and what did you see? What was the highest point in every town? Church, Cathedral, or abbey spires dominated the skyline. As the bright yellow `M´ is the McDonalds logo, the spire is the Church logo. The brand was visible everywhere.

These days commerce gets all our money and the Church almost nothing, so the spires have been overtaken by other buildings. The Church logo was the spire. Each spire showed a house of God. These days that's nothing, but in the time of Jesus, spires would have been as vulgar as neon. 'GOD IS HERE' says the spire. It was the biggest, boldest marketing ploy available in those days. Jesus used it to full effect with the excuse that they were reaching towards the heavens.

Perhaps excuse is not the right word here. Like any marketer, Jesus wanted to sell the reason for his spires. To say we want you to see it for miles and come with your cash would never work, so Jesus changed the focus of your attention to God; thereby selling you his concept.

"We can fill every town, village and city with a shop and make a fortune. People will see our spires and come from miles around to worship, to pray and to pay."

Nowadays other companies have followed Jesus. Mc Donalds have almost as big a coverage as he crafted for his company all those years ago. When every city, town and village that has a Church also has a McDonalds then the fast food giants have made it. They're getting pretty close – one in four Americans visit a McDonalds regularly. Of course, Jesus did dabble in fast food himself with the loaves and fishes, something we'll touch on in the next chapter.

Look at any city now and commerce is what reaches for the sky. Large corporations have towers built from the proceeds of the customer. Jesus started the trend with the customer giving money to the poor Church.

I love the way Jesus set up a profitable corporation which makes everyone feel sorry for the financial state of one of the richest organisations in the world. If you are in ever in Rome, nip round the Vatican with a calculator and add up the values of the treasures. You won't be able to include priceless artefacts, but you'll run out of digits in the first room. If you sold one or two of the trinkets in the Vatican museum you could wipe out the debt of a third world country. Funny how they haven't…

If you think the Church is poor then how did they ever manage to get some of the most magnificent buildings in the world built? Answer – great marketing and total knowledge of the psychology of the customer.

It is the 'money is bad' concept again. Evil money will stop you entering the kingdom of heaven, but the Church can put it to good use.

The first ever money laundering operation was run by Jesus.

He spiritually laundered your dirty evil money into good giving - save all - spiritually fine currency. The only difference is that when Jesus laundered your cash he kept it. Try doing that in New Jersey. Go on, convince a mafia don that he'll be spiritually cleansed when you keep his laundered cash. I dare you. Funny thing is when you die; the Jesus Corporation will be employed at the funeral service and I'm sure McDonalds won't be doing the catering.

McJesus serves a Happy Meal

Jesus had been having a really bad day. John the Baptist had been killed by King Herod and Jesus was gutted, so he went to the desert to clear his head. But being a celebrity, people followed him wherever he went. It was hard for him to be alone. 5000 fans followed him, like sheep. It's a bloody desert, there's nothing there. Come to think about it, sheep wouldn't have followed, they'd have known that they may starve to death due to the inhospitable desert conditions.

Jesus knew the people would come so he had a trick up his sleeve and a way to make more money and add to his celebrity-status.

There are 5000 people on a hill and the story says there are only five loaves and a couple of fish to go around. But do you really think a businessman with the commercial sense of Jesus would forget the catering?

The trick was to feed 5000 on no budget and make them feel they got something for nothing. Jesus was a wise man. He knew he was in a tight spot. If he flashed the cash around and sold tickets for his gigs, he'd have blown his cover as a poor preacher man. He had to find a way to cater his event with no cost to his organisation. He had it sponsored.

Each loaf and fish was donated by the event sponsors. In return, their produce was sampled by 5000 potential customers who would surely come back for more. They messed up the numbers a little and twelve full baskets were left over; but overall it was a success. It was the first real Happy Meal, (but, without the toy). The companies involved did not keep regular accounts; however, reports of the time stated that their profits rocketed following the event. It is not known if Jesus got a cut.

Sir Bob Geldof did a similar gig in July 1985 called
Live Aid where, out of nothing, a lot more than 5000
were fed. Jesus had done it first so Bob got much less
credit than he should have.

Sponsorship is one of the finest tools for any business. Getting someone else to pay for your service or
product is a true miracle. Burger King or Mc Donald's
free movie toys with the kids´ meals are an example.
You provide an addition to your product, a marketing
hook and you pay nothing.

Once you have your business model ready to go, re-
think your plan with tied marketing, co-promotions
and sponsorship. You will be amazed at what effect it
can have on your business. Jesus took his concept, sold
the belief and was unafraid of looking at every possible opportunity. That is why his business became so
successful.

As Jesus rolled into town, his band of followers themselves became a commodity. He created the first marketable audience, the cornerstone of modern media.
Media needs an audience to survive. Jesus created the
first organised media attraction.

Everyone wanted the, 'I've touched Jesus' T-shirt con-
cession or the blessed sandal stand.

A particular favourite at the time was the 'Bless Me
Quick' hats and the 'My other God is a Pagan' stickers.
Novelty walking sticks, which broke when thrown

down, were also a hit.

Lesson from Jesus:

Groups of people become an audience. This audience can be sold to advertisers for marketing, advertising or promotions.

Belief it or not

Most people only need to be given one reason not to proceed with a business plan. Funding, competition, product problems and just being told you will not succeed can be enough to torpedo anyone's plans. But winners, business leaders and Jesus himself made every obstacle into a challenge and found a way to proceed no matter how difficult it was. Although belief was funnily enough the business of Jesus, it is the cornerstone of success in any business.

Jesus was the master salesman. He sold you a belief stronger than anyone before, or since. He sold you fear. He sold you the unknown. It was amazing. He found a product which you have no way of knowing is true; the afterlife. No one has come back and said he's right or talking nonsense. We'd all love to think it's true but there is no real way of knowing. The unexplained was used by Jesus and his company to prove the existence of the afterlife. What a concept. I wish I could come up with something like that.

Give me your cash so that when you die you won't suffer in hell. Let us know if we're wrong and there'll be a full refund – NOT!

Look at the Church today. Competing with the mass media is tough but they still go on. People still get to a stage in life where they are scared not to have a belief. Electricians wouldn't change a plug for you without sending in a bill, yet they'll make sure the Church lights are all working, for no charge. The heating, plumbing, upholstery and carpentry are usually taken care of for no money or at an obscene discount. Why? Jesus scared them into it. What if they didn't do it? Would that be against the Church and like throwing sand in the face of the almighty? Think of the eternal damnation. Sod it, give me a stepladder and a 100 watt bulb, no charge - just in case.

Goodwill is a huge income for the Church. It's not something every business can capitalise on, however, the Church use it all the time. As a result it is saving them heaps of money. If we go back to the loaves and fishes, how do you think Jesus convinced the suppliers to sponsor the event? "Well don't bother guys, keep your fish, Satan will be waiting for you to welcome you to an eternity of damnation. See you later, lads; in fact no I won't because I'll be in my father's kingdom with all the riches of the world."

None of us will ever get such a great scam. Jesus was too good at the 'just in case' principle. People are selfish by nature. It's not a bad thing; it is the way nature intended. We have to look after number one because we are all we can ever truly depend on. We can never guarantee that family, friends and acquaintances won't let us down, but we know we will always be there for ourselves. To truly understand business we must understand the customer. We need to know what drives them to decisions, what they desire and which buttons to push for a response. Jesus was a master.

Say you have a new can of peas to sell. How do you drive the sale? Jesus would label them 'full of Godly goodness' or 'saviour peas'. He'd have them as symbols of God and offer redemption to those who ate them.

We're stuck in the real world with the potential customer. A vegetable eater is not quite enough, think more, is he or she well off, poor, what lifestyle do they have? Do they have children, a car and a home; do they go out at the weekend? Are they golfers? Do they have medical complaints?

Find out all you can about the customer and target them. For example, if there's a niche in the market for one legged pea eaters, then our peas will provide balance and stability. We market them as better than two legs. They can disguise your limp. Pop a one legged model into the advert and we have ourselves a winner. Every one legged pea eater on the planet would be on our side.

The same applies to anything you market. Be the customer. Walk a few miles in their moccasins and find out what they want. Make your customer believe that your product is what they need to have. Sales are driven by desire. People like to think it is their choice to buy, not yours. Once they feel it is their choice they will do the deed.

Jesus painted the picture of you joining his winning team where the rewards were unbelievable. He made you make the decision of wanting to be in his team.

Lesson from Jesus:

Good sales come from the desires of the customer. The customer has to believe they are in control of the decision to like your product or service.

Miracle Products

Miracles are great advertising. Jesus used these with great skill. He knew the unexplained would add to his reputation. It was pure show business. He is the Son of God and can do anything. Think of David Blaine cutting off his ear and the next day it was back, surely a modern miracle. Did you see the one where the magician asked someone to think of a special person, only to have the ash from a piece of paper mark their name on his chest? Now that must have been a miracle.

I remember the day after the last David Blaine show. How many times did I hear the phrase, "did you see that guy on TV last night?" Hundreds. Each time his potential video sales rocketed. I've seen him actually hover above the street. Once I learned how to do it, it was less of a miracle. Did Jesus use plants in the audience when he made cripples walk? Could the blind men see anyway? Whatever the answer, it didn't half make the word spread like wild fire. This man makes blind men see and heals the dying so he must have special powers. Jesus could've made the cripples walk out of sight of anyone else, but he chose to do it to impress the masses.

Imagine if you had turned up in 25 A.D. with a solar powered DVD player. Who'd be miracle man then? If your product or service can have that wow factor then it will sell. Give the customers something to remember you by; don't just go with the flow. If it's a shoe shop and you give free matching leather gloves with every pair of shoes, the word will soon get around: Especially with women who care about such things. Although I don't know why, I've never dated a woman and noticed her shoes. My eyes never seem to get down that far.

Good business is a lot like show business. Don't let the public see how the trick works, but give them something special to talk about. Leave them talking about you and wanting more.

It's all image marketing. If you have a simple corner shop, does it look clean and well maintained? If so, people will have faith that you won't go bankrupt. Do you have hand written price labels or neat typed ones? Everything sends a signal to the customer. You have to say what you are in every aspect of the business, from the colours and fabrics, to the cleanliness and layout.

•   Everything matters.

Be the customer and ask yourself what picture they build of you. Ask someone to tell you what image they get. If you run a pub and have entertainment on a Friday night, does the hand written poster do it justice or does it look cheap?

Get people talking about you in a good way, Make your own miracles.

Lesson from Jesus:

You must become the talking point.

Jesus of Nazareth

It was none too snappy a title. Funny thing that he knew about the 70s rock outfit back then, but Jesus of Nazareth knew he'd picked the wrong name. He had to drop the, 'of Nazareth' bit. It was too parochial. He was forced to look small by his name. He had to become Jesus. Many people make the same mistake of not making the business name fit the future prospects.

Even the great Richard Branson made a small mistake with the Virgin Atlantic Airline. As you head over the Indian Ocean, the Pacific etc you are on a UK-US named airline. However, in Richard's defence, few in the industry envisaged the airline lasting, let alone being the huge global success it has become.

Jesus dropped the clumsy title to become the one thing others have tried to follow: a one name icon. Elvis, Madonna, McDonalds, Bud are all global brands big enough for one name. The one name makes them seem even more powerful. Jesus, again, was a leader. He was the first.

Naming your business is one of the most important things you will ever do. You have to look at what your business plan is. Where do you see yourself in ten years? Will the name still be appropriate?

"I'm going to Hoover up."

"I need an aspirin."

"I'm wearing my Levis."

"Jesus, that's hot."

All examples of how brand names have become accepted generic vocabulary.

Avoid the mistake of naming your business after someone who might not be there in ten years and you will have to live with the ex wife/husband's name on your stationary and chequebook for ever...

Jesus the Leader

The business of Jesus was an early lesson to those who follow. His management style was perfect. He said 'this is the way' and his people followed. Even today his word is followed to the letter by his staff. That's how it should be. The boss calls the shots.

These days we have managers to manage teams, team leaders, supervisors and all sorts of middle men or women. One day big business will realise that middle management rarely works. These people often have no passion for the business but by being given power, they then hunger for more power not more sales or profit. They are not interested in driving the business, but only their own careers. They thrive on keeping the workers down and unhappy and keeping their own importance up and it kills the business.

Those on the shop floor are always more capable of identifying problems because they see them develop first-hand. They can recommend solutions and care about the company because they are in the thick of the action. Middle managers are removed from the action and will only put in place something they learned at college, which every other middle manager does too, making all companies into clones of each other with no entrepreneurial spirit left to drive a company forward on a new profitable course.

Those who know what is wrong in a business are often

the ones you pay the least money to. Those who interact with your customers often know how to make things work better. They get frustrated by managers giving them new instructions which they have never been consulted on. As a result, staff get demoralised in a job that's getting harder to do with tougher deadlines and targets.

Involve the people on the front line in your plans. Tell them what you want to achieve and get their suggestions. They feel valuable and important to the company and save you money on consultants and mistakes. By empowering them you gain their respect and their commitment to your business.

This seems simple but I've worked for one of the biggest financial organisations on the planet and they couldn't do this. Every month a manager would have a new impractical idea which only served to increase the turnover of staff not profits.

Try asking your employee questions:

- "How can we solve the problems we are having with quality?"

- "What could we do to help you be more efficient?"

Not everyone who works for peanuts is a fool. Some of your best consultants may already be on your payroll.

Jesus listened to his people, answered questions directly from his disciples and taught them his way. He also listened to their problems, concerns and issues and reassured them that he was steering them in the right direction. Jesus made sure the disciples ran his business as he would.

Jesus began the original franchise concept. He was able to see that expansion of his business was not something he was capable of alone. Like McDonalds, his managers trained with him to do things the same way everywhere. A Big Mac is a Big Mac is a Big Mac, whatever store you are in. Jesus started that concept. His business was duplicated all over the world HIS WAY every time. Build a business, but keep control of the things that matter. Make sure even though you are not on the premises, you are still running your business.

Remember, like Jesus, you dreamt of your success. Don't let anyone less passionate than yourself jeopardise what you've worked on. Expansion is a dangerous game mainly due to that phenomenon. The bigger your business becomes the less you are able to control all of it. You MUST, as Jesus did, install passion in your disciples and empower them to make the business succeed in the same way you would.

For every new level your business achieves, you should reflect on the control and influence you still have. Your business was your religion. Are you and your disciples still following the same faith? Are your disciples setting up an alternative sect? Make them believe in your faith, don't accept any alternatives because it is your business. They work for you and do what you pay them to do. Always have the disciples following you.

Your staff are valuable resources who have needs, desires, ambition and loyalty. Loyalty and appreciation are directly proportional. The less you appreciate your staff, the less loyal they will be to you.

Be wary of Judas. Everyone has a price, be it thirty pieces of silver, a promotion or revenge. Everyone has a point at which loyalty ends and survival takes over. Guard your secrets and trust only those who have earned it.

There is always someone ready to sell you down the river. Often this happens because you have undervalued an employee and they have reached a stale part of their career. The desire to succeed overtakes the weakening loyalty as they are continually ignored and are unappreciated.

How many managers dismiss the staff they employ as just numbers? Being treated as a robot often ensures employees complete their tasks as robots, clocking in like clockwork, rubber-stamping the work and clokking out like clockwork.

How much does it cost to employ someone motivated and enthusiastic about your business?

Less than it does to employ someone who is not enthusiastic.

Think about that for a minute.

It's cheaper to keep someone enthusiastic in your business than keep upping the salary to hold on to unenthusiastic staff.

How is it done?

Simple, by respect, consideration and involvement.

Make your employees feel like they matter to your business. Respect the fact that they sweat for your business. They're busy getting paid less than you to generate your salary. So many businesses forget this.

Gordon Bethune from Continental Airlines made a great point. He showed all his staff a watch and opened the case to show the inside. He asked them which part of the watch was not vital. Even the smallest cogs are needed to make the watch work.

The cleaner, the dogsbodies, the office junior are all cogs which drive the machine forward. Your business needs all these cogs to work smoothly.

What you must do is value every cog or one day you'll be missing a vital part of the machine.

Lessons from Jesus:

Loyalty is a two-way street.

Respect those who make you money.

The God, the Bad, and the Ugly

Marketing was always the strength of Jesus. He took the old scriptures, weaved his magic and presented his ideas to his followers. Much of what he taught was in the scriptures already but it is now all seen as the work of Jesus. Jesus and God became the father and son two man operation. Forget the old prophets. Nowadays in Church it's all "Jesus said..." He's made it all his own. These days the prophets would certainly have some sort of claim against Jesus. There would be lawsuits for copyright infringement and libel too.

God suddenly became the father of Jesus, the devil his enemy and the world his flock.

Jesus had done what any businessman craves; he made an industry his own. Think of fast food, what's the first brand name you can think of? 90% say McDonalds. What drink would you like with that? Do you say Coke or Pepsi? It's all in the ownership of the industry you are in. Make your company the leader and the brand which stands out from the rest of the pack.

Show your competitors to be bad and ugly. They are your devils. They are not your followers.

Competition can be healthy for any business. It makes sense to understand your competitor and decide whether they constitute a real threat now or in the future. What can you offer that they can't? What can you do better than your rival?

Make your followers believe that they are headed down the path to hell if they ever chose the devil and his products over you and yours.

Pitching your brand to the public with the right message is not that difficult. You just have to understand where your rival is targeting and then pitch your product/service to ensure your message is the better fit to your target market. You also need to make sure your message can win over your rival's customers.

•	Offer something different or new

•	Match the product quality to the correct market

Lesson from Jesus:

**Your strengths and your rival's weaknesses
should be recognised and promoted.**

Elvis, James Dean and Freddie from Queen

Death was the business of Jesus; he was backed into a corner to prove a point. His wonderful sales technique was for him to help you to get to the kingdom of heaven and to live forever in happiness. It was only a matter of time before he was asked to prove it. He was put on the spot. So what if he died? What would happen to the business?

Most businesses take on the personality of the founder. It was his or her dream; they had the vision and the ideas to make the business happen in the first place, if they are removed will the business still function in the same way? That depends on the business and the size of the personality.

Most businesses evolve from the ideas of the founder but once in the public domain can be easily copied, unless the business IS the founder. Other businesses can survive a change of leadership but if the leader is fundamental to the product or service then the business has to adapt to the change to survive.

Elvis was the business, he was the attraction, James Dean, too and Queen couldn't survive without Freddie Mercury but they were all able to follow the example of Jesus to achieve even greater riches after the leaders had died.

Jesus had the perfect solution – to be born again.

But what a business opportunity! The PR alone from the death of Jesus has been stronger than any other event in the history of our planet. It's still talked about all the time. Every year Christians still celebrate his re-birth.

Pontius Pilate had sentenced Jesus to death.

Once again Jesus prepared his business for the future. Resurrection appearances were in place and ready for the story to continue. Were they real or were people paid off to say they had seen him rise from the dead? Did they just believe so much in his sales pitch that they imagined it? We'll never know but once again it was a smart move by The Jesus Corporation.

Elvis died famous and before his time. There have been a number of sightings since his death. It is said he watched his own funeral from Graceland. He didn't get quite the resurrection coverage that Jesus did. Being first was always Jesus' advantage!

The resurrection enhanced the Son of God claim and further embedded the business of Jesus into the mind of everyone in the civilised world.

Now there could be no dispute, Jesus, like Elvis, Marilyn Monroe, JFK, James Dean and Princess Diana was special and would not be forgotten.

Lesson from Jesus:

Just when the public think it's all over, hit them with an encore.

Guilt-free God Please

Every business has to grow with the needs of the customer foremost in its mind. Thousands of years after the Jesus Corporation began; the needs of some of its customers had changed. They found certain aspects of their religion too restrictive for the modern times. They sought diet Church for a new generation.

On October 31, 1517, Martin Luther, a Catholic priest, nailed to the door of Wittenberg Cathedral in Germany his "95 Theses" attacking certain practices of the Roman Catholic Church. When he refused to apologize, the Church excommunicated him, and he went into hiding in fear for his life.

This simple act started the Reformation; Luther started a revolution that pitted Protestants against Catholics. Those who wanted to break away from Catholicism were just looking for something lighter and less strict.

Without getting too involved in the debate between the Protestants and Roman Catholics – both acknowledge the continuing presence of the Holy Spirit in the Christian community. Both look upon the Bible as a divinely inspired book through whose pages the authentic Word of God can be heard afresh by every generation. Both believe in the forgiveness of sins, the power of prayer, and the promise of everlasting life to those who place their trust in Christ; and both empty their pockets for the Church.

The Catholic Church is much better at getting money out of the congregation. All the offerings to various saints around the Chapel, the crosses, trinkets, ornaments, little Virgin Mary statues, Pope pictures, they have everything. Protestants are simple involved in the diet religion, God Lite.

Seems strange so many people die because of their beliefs when to me there is one significant difference. Protestants are just diet Catholics.

Just like ordering a burger at Religion King, have it your way. "I'll have spiritual guidance please, easy on the guilt and hold the offerings."

But what this shows is how the Church, like McDonalds, has developed a menu to suit all tastes. The new salad dishes at burger restaurants around the world have responded to the developing tastes and lifestyles of the people as the Church did with the introduction of the low calorie faith.

Jesus Corporation still brings in the cash. However, the Catholic Church were nuts not to embrace this diet religion themselves. It could have been one of their own like Coke and Diet Coke. This caused a splinter religion to be formed, the Pepsi of Christianity.
The Catholic Church, having sold themselves on the words of Jesus, was unable to take over this religion

and pocket the cash. The game would've been up if they had. Religion, remember, is not about money – or so they say!

Lesson from Jesus:

Keep in touch with your customers´ needs.

The Last Wine of a Condemned Man

Jesus knew his time was almost up. He wanted to spread his interests far and wide. He wanted to bring products into his business and develop a new income while he still had the opportunity. Even to the end, he was thinking and planning. He bet on the futures markets.

Nowadays, investments are commonplace. The best investments are those where growth can be assured. Investment is simply gambling; horse racing on companies. The best horse race to bet on is the one with one horse. That opportunity for Jesus came at the famous Last Supper. He was underlining a marketing message he had already shared with his faithful followers. He was promoting a product he had a financial stake in: wine.

Jesus chose to change water into wine to give wine sales a boost. He marketed wine as the Holy alternative to water. After all, he could have changed water into almost anything, but he chose to make a statement. On the third day there was a wedding in Cana of Galilee, and the mother of Jesus was there. Now, both Jesus and his disciples were invited to the wedding. And when they ran out of wine, the mother of Jesus said to Him, "They have no wine." - John 2:1 – 11

Mary, full of the 'spirit' of the wedding, egged Jesus on to show his followers a trick.

Now there were set there six waterpots of stone, containing twenty or thirty gallons apiece. Jesus said to them, "Fill the waterpots with water". And they filled them up to the brim. And he said to them, "Draw some out now, and take it to the master of the feast". And they took it. When the master of the feast has tasted the water that was made wine, the master of the feast called the bridegroom. And he said to him, "You have kept the good wine until now!". - John 2:1 - 11

For some, changing water into wine was just a cheap trick. Jesus, however, knew that word would spread from the wedding at Cana to the world. Wine was elevated above water as the drink of choice for the Holy. When it came to the last supper, Jesus again underlined that message.

"Drink from it, all of you. This is my blood of the covenant, which is poured out for many for the forgiveness of sins. I tell you, I will not drink of this fruit of the vine from now on until that day when I drink it anew with you in my Father's kingdom." When they had sung a hymn, they went out to the Mount of Olives (and planted some grape seeds). - Matthew 26

The Church Hanteillan estate is mentioned by Pope Alexander III among the properties of Vertheuil Abbey, in 1179. In fact, one of the vineyards of the chateau is still called Vatican. Until twenty years ago, this vineyard produced a wine sold under the name 'Tour du Vatican'. I'm sure this is just coincidence.......

Jesus had a very powerful sales pitch. 'Whoever eats my flesh and drinks my blood has eternal life, and I will raise him up at the last day'. - John 4:13

Investing in that vineyard would be like betting on a one horse race.

Examine what Jesus did. He promoted wine, created a market and the Church invested in vineyards. He knew he would create a demand and anticipated the rise in sales. Once again, Jesus had shown incredible foresight and the Church incredible returns.

Jesus Jewellery

I've often wondered why the Church uses the cross as a symbol. James Dean fans and Princess Diana followers don't have twisted car wreckage around their necks, do they?

Somehow, Jesus dying for our sins means he can get the merchandising out without it being frowned upon. No one else could ever have carried this off. Imagine the Elvis hamburger necklace, the Isadora Duncan scarf, a Kurt Cobain shotgun pendant. Can you envisage the day you would wear a Buddy Holly Beechcraft Bonanza tie-pin? A Steve Irwin stingray brooch? A Kirsty McColl speedboat charm? Yet you may well wear a crucifix. How odd!

Was this another burst of genius from Jesus? Of course it was. Jesus was promoting the Jesus Corporation (JC) which sold the concept of death. What better to keep the dream alive than using the symbol of his passing as the symbol for his company.

This symbol reminds us that Jesus led the way, via the cross and his death, to the Kingdom of Heaven. The cross advertises the Church and the business He created.

As a symbol, the cross beats most other logos. Cheap, easy to reproduce (two sticks will do) and unforgettable. It had, in fact been used before.

In Scandinavia, the Tau cross symbolized the hammer of the God Thor. In Babylon, the cross with a crescent moon was the symbol of their moon deity. In India, in Hinduism, the vertical shaft represents the higher, celestial states of being; the horizontal bar represents the lower, earthly states. In Assyria, the corners of the cross represented the four directions in which the sun shines.

In Egypt, the ankh cross (a Tau cross topped by an inverted tear shape) is associated with Maat, their Goddess of Truth. It also represents the sexual union of Isis and Osiris. In Europe, the use of a human effigy on a cross in the form of a scarecrow has been used from ancient times. In prehistoric times, a human would be sacrificed and hung on a cross. The sacrifice would later be chopped to pieces; his blood and pieces of flesh were widely distributed and buried to encourage the crop fertility.

– http://www.religioustolerance.org

The Church should really be selling T-shaped trinkets. In Roman times the type of cross thought to be used for crucifixion was shaped like the letter 'T', unlike the traditionally depicted 'Latin cross'. This is now known as St. Anthony's Cross.

Jesus will always be associated with the Latin cross, examples of which are available at the Vatican gift shop and jewellers worldwide.

You will probably never get an image as powerful as the cross for your business. The McDonalds 'Golden Arches' is almost as simple but just not as hard-hitting.

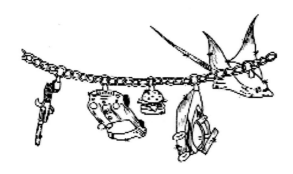

False Profits

One thing the Bible does tell us very clearly is to avoid false profits. (The spelling in the good book is terrible).

What are false profits? They are the imagined future profits of your business after a little success.

It's funny how so many businesses fall into the same traps. Managers, encouraged by a little success think they are wearing a fail-proof suit. They hold their head so high that they can't hear the little people on the shop floor anymore. Some people take their own importance to an even greater level. A word of caution for those that do. Your own anus is a poor conductor of sound. When you have your head up your ass, no one can hear you and you can't hear anything but wind and your own pathetic rumblings.

We can't all have the magical powers that the Son of God, or God himself is said to have, but, omnipresence is helpful when running a successful business. You have to know what the customer wants every day. You cannot do that from your own anus. Sure, it can be great to spend a month in Barbados on the hard-earned cash, but while you sip another Martini, back at the business things are falling apart because you're not on top of things.

Remember there is only one God in the Bible and one Jesus. There can only be one God in your business, you. Beware of managers you put in place to run the ship when you are away. They attempt a 'you' impersonation, usually very badly. Elvis impersonators are never quite Elvis, no one else is ever you.

One of the worst things that can happen to your business is letting someone take charge who thinks they know everything. Jesus listened to his followers. Middle managers often only listen to the sound of their own voice.

I once worked in a company where a new manager took over. He had his ideas and went with them no matter what anyone said to him. He was like a steamroller over a hamster on a marble floor. His steamroller tactics meant that most people were too scared to say that he was wrong. He also told everyone everything, because he liked to hear sound coming out of his mouth. What he didn't realise was that what he said was repeated in every office in the building, so when he started telling one person one thing and another the opposite, as he often did, his credibility dissolved before his eyes.

If you surround yourself with yes men, don't ever expect the truth. You'll only ever get a yes. Jesus surrounded himself with people who questioned his faith, his ideas and him. The Bible is full of references to Jesus answering his doubters. If someone asked Jesus why, he had to find an answer, this helped him to evolve his business. It made him question himself.

When you fill out any business plan, you have to indicate your strengths, weaknesses, opportunities and threats. The SWOT test is standard. Try asking a yes man if you have any weaknesses or threats. I doubt that they will be honest.

Some of the wealthiest entertainers in the world have been put in the poor house by yes men. They want to buy a mansion/jet/racehorse which they can't afford and ask a yes man if it can be bought. He says yes, he's on the payroll to say yes. How did a yes man get on the payroll?

He was employed by a man who liked the sound of his own pathetic rumblings.

The Power and the Glory

Most entrepreneurs are needy. They seek the power or the glory of running their own business, often both.

You can use this to your advantage when dealing with other entrepreneurs. Do they seek to see their name in lights? Visit Atlantic City and the huge TRUMP signs will tell you what 'The Donald' needs. We could drop deep into psychology and ask why he needs to prove himself like this, but that's a whole other book. The main thing is to realise that his constant need to prove himself drives him forward.

How is this advantageous for an entrepreneur dealing with this type of businessman? His needs are also his weakness. When you understand his needs you can do as Jesus did and use the needs of others to help your business.

Jesus always understood the needs of everyone around him. He understood his followers, his disciples and his doubters. By satisfying other people's needs you are able to distract them from your goals. You can also improve their perception of you at the same time. Jesus gave people what they wanted to hear, a true hope and a reason to have faith.

If you are dealing with someone in business, assess their needs and adjust your pitch to ensure you use their weakness against them. A little preparation and research will put you in a stronger position.

The Power and the Glory are often weaknesses which you can exploit in others. Be aware that your actions are also assessed by everyone as Jesus was assessed. Be careful of assuming you are more powerful and important than you really are. Jesus, as a humble man, achieved much more than any other man in history.

Forever and Ever

Longevity in business is not easy. Whilst Jesus was successful both in life and in the legacy he left, there are millions who have tried and failed to replicate his success.

Jesus had the vision, the marketing and the ability to make his business work. His genius drove his vision forward; he kept control of every aspect of the business and ensured those who took over control of his business did it his way. All of these steps are important. If one step is missed, the longevity of your business is compromised.

We have touched on many critical points in establishing and running a successful business and we have touched on some of the failings of many of the businesses with which you come into contact.

Failure is the easiest option. Jesus had faith. Without faith in yourself and your idea, you will never be able to build any business. Jesus promoted absolute belief. The slightest shred of doubt in your own talent will slowly eat away your enthusiasm and capability.

Like Jesus, you must be humble and accept your place on earth. Once you believe your own hype, you are doomed. If you believe you can walk on water then your feet will get wet. The public face of your business has to be larger than life and stronger than steel.

Your own public image has to be the same. Do not confuse this image with the business or yourself. Your business, however large, is fragile.

Many of the biggest businesses in the world have been days away from bankruptcy but the public profile has never wavered. Accept your humble, vulnerable status and you will be sure to protect your business. Without labouring the points too much, respect those who work for you and respect your customers.

Without respect for your workers, your business will crumble from the inside. A simple thanks is often all the appreciation they need. Your thanks will mean nothing unless it is sincere. No matter how big your business, it is easy to find out the names of the people on the shop floor before you meet them. The impression that can leave in the worker can be as good as a pay rise.

Always remember that those who work for you make you wealthy. Remember that every day or they'll be making someone else wealthy. When they leave you, they will most likely go directly to your competitors with your working methods in their head.

Your customers deserve respect. As simple as this may sound, often companies forget that feeling they had when they made their first sale. After writing the business plan, raising the capital, finding premises, hiring staff and finally starting the business, it is almost relief that greets the first customer. Every customer should be respected like that first customer.

The fact that you've sold a million items a week does not mean that each customer is not important. Each and every sale you make is as important as that first sale, for you, your workers and your bottom line.

Jesus respected his followers and cared about each one of them. By doing this, he created a mutual respect and formed a relationship with his customers. Customer relations are just that: relationships. Relationships never work without respect and trust being built up. You have to build and maintain that relationship with your customers. Do not betray their trust; be honest in your dealings with them. Respect the intelligence of the customer; they have the right to chose to go elsewhere and will if you don't give them the respect that they deserve.

Being humble will enable you to generate a natural respect for those around you.

Lesson from Jesus:

Be humble and respect those around you.

It's all There in Writing

If you aren't yet convinced about the theory of this book, perhaps you should pick up the best-selling book on the planet – the Bible. It contains all the evidence you need. The first thing in school you are taught is The Lord's Prayer. It really is very funny indeed. Jesus was having a laugh with us at our expense. He loved the confessional line, "Give us this day our daily brea.". Bread as we all know is slang for money.

Jesus meant give us this day YOUR daily bread.

"It is more blessed to give than receive." - Acts 20:35

Yeah, but it seems Jesus wanted us to be the givers and the Church the receivers. Who exactly did he want you to give to? The poor, but with the funds strategically channelled through the Church.

Think of what Jesus said: "Repent, for it is better that a man find a cup of water in the age that is coming than all the riches of the world." - Coptic Apocryphal Gospel.

Now think of a stockbroker telling you about the next big thing. He makes you feel like he knows what's about to happen, has more knowledge than you and convinces you to invest his way. "Invest in oil because there is a shortage on the way." Jesus did the same. He's saying give us your money because with what's on the way you'll not need money.

Read it again. "Repent, for it is better that a man find a cup of water in the age that is coming than all the riches of the world." In the meantime, as you look for the water, the Jesus Corporation is out buying more gold with your hard-earned cash. He was the master salesman. On one hand, he offered us all the riches of the Kingdom of Heaven. On the other hand, being rich was frowned upon whilst you had a pulse.

If you ever need to find a way to run any business, Jesus will show you the way. The best information the Bible presents for any business is that of spreading the word, advertising and getting the message across. In any business it is the most important aspect. Whether you are communicating with the customers, suppliers or staff of the business, they have to understand the business through your preaching. Preach until they make your business part of their life and live by your commandments.

Millions have seen the Bible as a guidebook through life, but in actual fact, Jesus gave us the best guide to business there is. It showed:

- Planning - Prophets show us it was all planned
- Investment - Three wise men
- Marketing - Loaves and fishes
- Sales - The Church

Whatever the state of your business, simplify your

thinking and go back to the basics of business. Ask yourself the basic questions everyday.

- Do people still want what you offer?

- Is there still sufficient demand?

Remember that, prayer in business may help too.

A Prayer

Our investor, who art in leverage,
Hallowed be thy Name.
Thy customers come,
Thy will be done,
From service they have been given.
Give me this day your daily bread,
And forgive us our competitors,
As we forgive those who compete against us.
And lead us not into bankruptcy,
But deliver us from poor.
For cash is the King,
And the Power,
And the Glory,
Forever and ever,
Amen.

The Ten Business Commandments

1. My business shall be number one; no other business shall take its place.

2. My business identity and ideas shall be protected by copyright.

3. I shall ask my customers every day if they are still satisfied with my offerings.

4. My image will be true to the image of my business.

5. My employees will be respected and valued.

6. I will ensure the expansion of my business retains the true faith of the business plan.

7. I will seek followers in management who see the business as I do.

8. My business will become the talking point of its type.

9. I will continue to preach the gospel of my company through marketing and advertising.

10. My faith in myself will be strong.

A Final Word

I started this book because I saw that Church spires are higher than almost anything else in most small towns. In larger cities, banks or huge corporations reach for the sky.

I began to think about that. Was money behind it all?

This book started from there, as a tongue-in-cheek look at the Church and what could be learned for any business from its example.

The funny thing is, I never had a strong faith, and for me the Church was not cool. I couldn't find a space for it in my life.

I find myself now thinking what a seriously clever guy Jesus was, and how he did more to teach us all than the Church would ever promote. Jesus is cool. You don't have to be religious or follow a faith to see how the Church can teach us something about business.

I hope this book has helped you find a path to follow for your business.

I'd like to thank Donald Trump for his inspiration and the late Sir Reo Stakis for his kind words.

Business by Jesus

Written by

Kevin Cameron

~ Business By Jesus ~